Pink Lemonade

By: Lisa Michelle Grate

PATASKITY PUBLISHING CO.

Published By: Pataskity Publishing Company
Pataskity Publishing (USA) LLC
207 Hudson Trce Suite 102
Augusta, GA 30906

Pataskitypublishing.com

ISBN: 978-1-948605-19-9

It is our mission to build lifelong connections. Your thoughts, hopes, prayers, and stories are important to us. It is our mission to transform your publishing dreams into reality.

Copyright © 2020 Lisa Michelle Grate. All rights reserved. No portion of this book may be reproduced mechanically, electronically, or by any other means, including photocopying, without written permission of the author. It is illegal to copy this book, post it on a website, or distribute it by any other means without permission from the author.

About Lisa Michelle Grate

Lisa Michelle Grate is a resident of Dunbar Community of Georgetown, South Carolina, and a native of Andrews, South Carolina. She is the wife of Willie Grate Jr., a mother of three handsome sons and a soon-to-be grandmother. Grate is an entrepreneur of almost thirty years. She is the owner of Hair It Is Beauty Salon and Grate Affairs and Events by Lisa Michelle. She actively works in her church and community. Grate has a love for people and feels she meets no stranger. Her full-time employment is with the Georgetown County School District as a paraprofessional, and she loves it wholeheartedly.

Dedications

This book is in loving memory of my mother, Julia Lee Chandler-Williams (March 15, 1947- September 13, 2017).

This book is dedicated to my loving grandmother, Edna Rouse-Chandler (August 20, 1926- August 10, 2020).

This book is dedicated to my loving and supportive husband and children, my family, and friends.

Thanks to each of you who extended your love, kindness, prayers, and support to me.

Table of Contents

Topic: Prayer Is the Key	12
Week 1	13
Week 2	16
Week 3	20
Week 5	23
Week 4	26
Week 6	29
Week 7	32
Week 8	35
Week 9	38
Week 10	41
Week 11	44
Week 12	47
Week 13	50
Week 14	53
Week 15	56
Week 16	59
Week 17	62
Week 18	65
Week 19	68
Week 20	70
Week 21	74
Week 22	77
Week 23	80
Week 24	83
Week 25	86
Week 26	89
Week 27	92
Week 28	95
Week 29	98

Week 30 101
Week 31 104
Week 32 107
Week 33 110
Week 34 113
Week 35 116
Week 36 119
Week 37 122
Week 38 125
Week 39 128
Week 40 131
Week 41 134
Week 42 137
Week 43 140
Week 44 143
Week 45 146
Week 46 149
Week 47 152
Week 48 155
Week 49 158
Week 50 161
Week 51 164
Week 52 167
Conclusion 170

Prayer Is the Key

"Pray Without Ceasing" 1 Thessalonians 5:17

One of the most important lessons that I have learned in all my fifty years of life is that whatever comes your way, you make the best of it! I felt I was handed a huge basket of lemons but instead of looking at them as sour and bitter, I decided to add some sugar and make some lemonade, *Pink Lemonade*.

1 Thessalonians 5:17 teaches us that we should pray without ceasing, which means always pray if we want to defeat Satan. Prayer is essential to our greatness in life and destiny. We must learn the only to see the best in every situation is to be in prayer. Why do we need to pray always? Because the devil is not resting on his oars, he moves around looking for whom to destroy. I pray you will not become his victim in Jesus's name; hence, we must always pray as a believer in Christ Jesus. Do not forget that God will not come down to do what He had equipped us to do for us; that is why He said: "pray without ceasing." Until you pray, all things stay. Understand this and run fast with this truth.

- "Prayer turns your lemons into lemonade."

Lisa Michelle Grate

Week 1

Topic: God's Word Is A Light

"Thy Word Is A Lamp Unto My Feet And A Light For My Path."

Psalm 119:105

David teaches that God's word is a lamp; Through the scripture, we understand that God is the giver of direction; He is a way maker, and his word is a light to our pathway. Today I had my yearly mammogram. It was initially scheduled for August 27. I tried to move the date up earlier, but that did not happen. I know that in the midst of each challenge, God's word is my strong tower. I have learned that when we cherish God's word and believe in it, he will always guide us in all of our actions. If you want to have a fulfilled and colorful destiny, learn to believe in God's word.

The word of God lightens up every area of darkness in our lives and paves the way for our upliftment. It also makes us victorious over every situation and circumstance of life. Knowing God's word helps us to not sin against God.

In conclusion, let us take in more interest in God's word as it is our passport is to victory in life and destiny. As we delight in God's word, we should allow the Holy Spirit to use it to give us direction in life. We should be obedient to the spirit's dictate because God will lead us through our inward man the Holy Spirit as we learn to believe all His promises in the word concerning us.

Pink Lemonade

How often do you read God's word? You cannot progress beyond the level of scripture that dwells in your heart. God's Word will become a light and a lamp to your path.

Pink Lemonade

Week 2

Topic: Trust Him Totally

"Trust In The Lord With All Thine Heart, And Lean Not Unto Thine Own Understanding."

Proverb 3:5

After my husband left for work at 3:00 a.m., I moved to his side of the bed to be close to the fan due to having a hot flash. Once I woke up, I felt very sore on my right breast. I immediately thought to myself: "Boy, did I sleep badly." I immediately checked for any abnormalities, and to my surprise, I felt a lump that I had not even noticed before. I did an exam (self) two days before scheduling my mammogram. After several checks, I called my sister, who advised me to go straight to the Emergency Room and let them do further testing. Upon arrival, I was met by a very compassionate doctor who treated me as family. He immediately scheduled an exam for the next day, followed by an ultrasound, and called the breast doctor to schedule an appointment.

During this process, I often reflected on this scripture. I could hear my mom singing about trusting in Jesus. The scripture states that we should put our trust in God and not in man. Do not forget the scripture says cursed is everyone who trusts man: "Cursed is the one who trusts in man, who depends on flesh for his strength and whose heart turns away from the Lord (Jeremiah 17:5).

God is saying that we should shift our minds away from man and look up to him only as of the giver of all things, which truly He is.

The Word of God is teaching us that whatever height we attained, it is by God's help, not by our power or understanding. Praise God!

The benefit you derived from trusting in thy Lord is enormous; I will highlight some:

1) It keeps you in fellowship with God.

2) It delivers you from the worship of men.

3) It makes your blessing a lasting one.

4) It keeps your faith alive.

5) The joy of thy Lord shall be your strength.

Do you trust in God? Explain. It pays to trust in God!

Pink Lemonade

Week 3

Topic: Prayer Is The Key

"Pray Without Ceasing."

1st Thessalonians 5:17

Prayer changes all things; It brings us to fellowship with God.

Today I tried to focus on my work. Being an event planner, I had to set up for a graduation party and a baby shower, but all I could do was think to myself. I realized I could not stress myself out, so I continued to work and spoke good things into the atmosphere.

The scripture teaches us that we should pray without ceasing, which means we should always pray.

I took a moment and said a prayer to God for strength and peace. Sometimes in life, God allows us to have family and friends to pray with us. Other times, we have to pray over our lives and our destinies individually. Either way, God hears us, and he a rewarder of those who diligently seek him. I felt renewed after I said a prayer, and I continued my day with a smile on my face.

Pink Lemonade

How often do you pray?

Pink Lemonade

Week 4

Topic: Brand New

"Therefore, If Any Man Be In Christ, He Is A New Creature: Old Things Are Passed Away: Behold, All Things Become New."

2nd Corinthians 5:17

As I sit thinking about what diagnosis I will get from my doctor regarding having been told I have breast cancer, I cannot help but think of my mother whom also had a cancer diagnosis. I prayed and cried, then cried and prayed, and still, I have to remind myself that God will see me through.

The moment we accept the Lord Jesus as our Lord and Savior, we are not the same as we use to be. Something changed in us, and it is a mystery that no one can explain. It is not a must for you to be able to explain, but it has happened.

God is saying here that there at redemption, we are no more the same as we use to be. Our sins are cleared, and a new life begins immediately, there is no more condemnation to them who are in Christ Jesus; therefore, we should learn to forget our past ways of life before we get saved and start focusing on our redemption right in Christ Jesus.

Do you believe in what God says? Do you believe that all things are now new for you? Are you still flowing in the realm of your past?

Pink Lemonade

Week 5

Topic: Stand Firm And Love

"Be On Guard—Stand Firm In The Faith. Be Courageous. Be Strong. And Do Everything With Love. 1st Corinthians 16:13

Today is a follow-up with my family doctor, and after covering what I initially came in for I advised him that I had a pending biopsy from an irregular mammogram, so he checked the status, and though it was still pending, he assured me that he would call me the following day to let me know the results.

There is a need for us always to be moving guard as a believer.

The devil is our greatest adversary. He is doing everything within his power to ensure that we drawback in the faith.

But then for us not to be his victim, we have to put on our guard spiritually, and physically. We have to stand firm in the faith and be courageous in all things we do through the holy spirit's help.

What behaviors do you practice that results in your faith being strong?

Pink Lemonade

Week 6

Topic: What Motivates Your Action?

"And Whatever You Do, Do It Heartily As To The Lord And Not To Men."

Colossians 3:23

I woke up early this morning to shower and prepare for my work day. Shortly after 9:00 a.m., I received a call from my doctor informing me that my results were in from the biopsy and that it was indeed cancer, and that is all the information that he could share with me until I met with the breast doctor on the following Tuesday. I immediately left out of the salon to go inside the house to gather my thoughts.

We should be diligent about God's work, do it well and be mindful that God is watching our actions; rather, they are big or small. He comes quickly to pay every man according to what his works shall be.

Does faith motivate your actions?

Pink Lemonade

Week 7

Topic: Where Is Your Heart Focusing?

"For Where Your Treasure Is, There Will Your Heart Will Be Also."

Luke 12:34

Today is the big day for my cousin Sophia's wedding! I purposed in my heart to not think about this upcoming Tuesday when I go to the doctor but to focus on making her wedding as beautiful as she can imagine. Although my mind would often reflect on my circumstance, I had a great time with family and friends. Jesus taught His disciples to be mindful of where they put their treasures as they continue in this earthly journey. My mind reflected on this scripture. Decorating has always been a joy to me, but my greatest treasure and delight are in God.

Jesus provides these teachings so that we would know to focus and invest more in the things of the spirit, which has eternal reward than the material things of this world that is for a while. Looking at it in the physical when you want to know what a man mostly cherished look at what he invests in, his investment reflects where his heart will be.

But in our text today, we are advised to lay up treasures for ourselves in heavenly places where no cankerworm can destroy, and as we invest more in heavenly things Our attention will be more up there, having that hope and assurance that one day we will see our Father and be with him where he is. Brethren begin to lay up treasure in things of the spirit than on earthly things that will perish.

Are you spiritually focused? Is your attention on your circumstance or on God?

Pink Lemonade

Week 8

Topic: No Limitation

"I Can Do All Things Through Christ Who Strengthens Me." Philippians 4:13

Today, after sending our sons off to Sunday School, my husband and I talked about my situation and decided that whatever came out, we would fight it with everything in us. In the scripture, Paul reminds us that everything is possible for him by the strength of Jesus Christ.

The Apostle Paul was saying that he couldn't have achieved greatly in ministry if not for God's help. He said everything is possible for him by the strength of Jesus Christ.

Now that I am only one day away from visiting the doctor, my nerves really got the best of me. I had to keep myself busy to ease my mind! God, please, I asked: "See me through this ordeal."

As a believer, we should continuously be affirmed that Christ is the giver of every good and perfect gift. His works are great as he manifests through us. We are just a vessel God uses to do it. I believe this will humble us not to be proud because if we are God himself. Let us learn to subscribe all glory to Him for what He had done through us and what He is still going to do.

Nothing is impossible for a true child of God, praise God! Do you see yourself as God sees you? Explain.

Pink Lemonade

Week 9

Topic: All Of My Needs Will Be Met

"My God Shall Supply All Your Need According To His Riches In Glory By Christ, Jesus."

Philippians 4:19

Today is the day my appointment is scheduled with my breast doctor to discuss my biopsy results. After waiting for a few minutes, the doctor comes in, and the first thing he says is: "If you can hear me out for about thirty minutes, you will be alright." I then began to listen to him as he described my situation and the plans he had to help me get through this, a surgery followed by both Chemotherapy and Radiation. He had a genuine concern for my well-being and assured me that the situation would be fixed through surgery and treatments.

Our God is still in the business of meeting his children's needs; The truth of the matter is that there will be no lack for them who love God and a rod walking according to His purpose and dictate in life.

In our text, the Apostle Paul talked to the church through the Holy Spirit's inspiration that God will supply all our needs according to His riches in glory by Christ Jesus. The question is, how great is the glory of our God? Can anybody tell me how exactly it is? We cannot say it exactly, but we know that God's glory is immeasurable, indescribable, so that is to the magnitude our need shall be met praise God!

How great is the glory of our God? Describe the greatness of God in your life?

Pink Lemonade

Week 10

Topic: God Has Great Plans For Us

"For I Know The Plans I Have For You, Declares The Lord Plans To Prosper You And Not To Harm You, Plans To Give You Hope And A Future."

Jeremiah 29:11

Today my surgery was scheduled, and I can honestly say that I feel relief from worrying! The tumor size was estimated to be very small, and my diagnosis is early pre-stages, not even stage two. Thinking back to one year ago this time. I was still mourning the death of my mother, who transitioned to be with Jesus on September 13, 2017. Although she was battling stage 4 Pancreatic Cancer, her death was unexpected because she was doing so well. In fact, the day she got sick, she walked into the ER expecting to get treated and return home. Little did we know, she was getting better to go to her Heavenly Home.

God's plans for his creation are perfect, good, and the best. He never meant evil for us. His thoughts and plans are the best. Look at that text we read; His plans are to prosper us and not harm us, give us hope and a future.

Believers should learn to believe in God's plans for them; we should know that He loves us, and He wants us to prosper in all our endeavors.

No matter what is happening, believers should always declare God's written word concerning them and not what they see happening because what we see is temporal, but the word of God is eternal.

Pink Lemonade

Do you trust God with your future? Explain.

Pink Lemonade

Week 11

Topic: Peace Is Guaranteed In Christ

"You Keep Him In Perfect Peace Whose Mind Is Stayed On You Because He Trusts In You."

Isaiah 26:3

Today I have an event to set up! I love what I do, and I am always excited to do anything I put my hands to do, but this stress for my diagnosis is taking its toll on me. Despite it all, God will see me through!

Trusting in the supremacy of God is the gateway to perfect peace in life. Trusting in God means us holding on and trusting in Him for all our human and spiritual needs.

A believer should learn to trust and abide in Christ, for the Peace of God to multiply in their life, when we fail to trust in Him we ran into the hand of Satan and it agents because we could not wait on Him to perform that which He had promised us, therefore, looking our Peace. There should say nothing on earth that worth us losing our Peace in Christ Jesus; this is a treasure which God had given us His children, so let us treasure it. How will you not lose the Peace of God? By you trusting in Jesus Christ absolutely for all things, He cares so much for you. Hallelujah!

Pink Lemonade

Have you experience God's peace being perfect? Explain.

Pink Lemonade

Week 12

Topic: Ask And It Will Be Given

"If Any Of You Lack Wisdom, Let Him Ask God, Who Gives Generously To All Without Reproach, And It Will Be Given To Him."

James 1:5

Today is Sunday, and I'm excited to go to Sunday School to get and study the word. The church is what I need the most, especially in a time such as now and I will continue to worship God through song and praise.

We need God's wisdom to survive in life; without wisdom, we are sure to fail.

In the scripture, the question is asked: "Is their anyone that lacks wisdom?" I believe you know it is possible for some folks not to have the spirit of wisdom. God said they should ask.

The scripture states: "Wisdom is the principal thing, therefore get wisdom." Without it, you cannot profit from God's word. Today, I urge you to get wisdom, and the true wisdom is from God, so why not ask Him today since he had promised He would release it to those in need? Gory is to God in the highest!

How often do you pray? Do you use moments of prayer to ask God for his wisdom?

Pink Lemonade

Week 13

Topic: It Is Good To Praise God

"Oh, Those Men Would Praise The Lord For His Goodness And For His Wonderful Works To The Children Of Men!"

Psalm 107: 8

While some people may choose to worry, I chose not to worry. Today, I decided to stay busy with my boys, who are so supportive and uplifting to me. We enjoyed our lunch date that was much needed.

When times are good or even when times are bad, we still should praise God.

One may ask: "Why should we praise Him?

Praise God for His goodness and all His wonderful works. When we praise God, we extend the invitation to God to do more for us, so let praising God be our way of God love such. As we begin to give God quality praise, He is set to do more for us. Praise Jesus! He loves when His children praise Him.

Do you praise God? How often do you praise God? Why do you praise him?

Pink Lemonade

Week 14

Topic: God Is Dependable

"For He Satisfied The Thirsty And Fills The Hungry With Good Things. "Psalm 107:9

I realize that until sickness hits you, you really cannot begin to imagine what one goes through. As my summer vacation comes to an end, I look forward to meeting the twenty little people who will become my family for the next ten months. August 15, we had our staff meet and greet for the upcoming year. I love my students, and often they make me laugh or smile. It is amazing how God always satisfies us not with the big things alone but also with the smaller things in life; Such experiences are actually big!

We know that our God is Jehovah Jireh, the provider, all that we need and will ever need is in His hand, just according to our text; "For he satisfied the thirsty and filled the hungry with good things." The hope is that we serve God. He is the ever dependable, and despite your need, He has it in His hands.

Whatever your needs are, come to Him. He has much of it with Him praise God!

Let us forget that the keyword to receiving from God is your faith. Your ability to believe God in His Word every day of your life, as you do this, you have a sign in for a life of victory. Praise God!

Do you trust God with everything rather it seems big or small? Explain.

Pink Lemonade

Week 15

Topic: It Will Come Back To You

"Do Not Be Deceived: God Cannot Be Mocked. A Man Reaps What He Sows."

Galatians 6:7

Today, Mrs. Cumbee and I will tackle getting our classroom prepared for the babies' comfort! We met many of the children and their families and boy do we anticipate a long and busy year. I vowed to take care of these precious little children who enters our class.

In life, whatever a man sows the same will he reap. YOU SOW well; you will reap. You cannot confuse God with your confession. He is not confused. So let us be careful how we go about life and what we do therein because one day, we shall reap what sow, and you know the amazing thing? Our harvest will surely be more than what we sow. So be careful!

In the text, we read today God is saying to us that He cannot be deceived, and mind you our God is alpha and omega; He knows all, so we cannot mock Him, we cannot deceive Him, we cannot get Him to confuse instead we confuse ourselves.

Many do not believe that there will be repercussions, not knowing that they are sowing a seed that will soon grow and reap if abundantly.

Pink Lemonade

What kind of seed are you sowing? Don't forget you shall reap it either in the long run or short run, but you will surely reap it. Be careful!

Pink Lemonade

Week 16

Topic: The Good Shepherd

"The Lord Is My Shepherd"

Psalm 23

I woke up this morning with a feeling like no other! For the first time in weeks, I feel reassured that my God will see me through! I will go through this day, reminding myself that my God can do anything!

A good father ensures that all the needs of his children are met. That is how our God is. Look at the Bible passage we read earlier. It states: "The Lord is my shepherd. I shall lack nothing." We are all children in God's hands.

Our God is always there to lead and direct us so that we will not fall into the ditch of life: the gospel truth. Praise God!

Do you understand that God is your shepherd? How do you apply this scripture to your life?

Pink Lemonade

Week 17

Topic: The Sworn Blessing

"Surely Goodness And Mercy Shall Follow Me All The Days Of My Life, And I Shall Dwell In The House Of The Lord Forever."

Psalm 23:6

Often, I reflect on my mother! She always instilled in me that there is nothing too hard for God. Even in my going through, I give him glory. Psalms 23 was one of her favorite scriptures.

When God says, "Surely," it means nothing can change His blessings for His children. It is a great and good thing to serve God! Look at all these blessings He had blessed us with. What a great God we served!

God's blessing is unchangeable, more, more so when He said surely the scripture said He spake and it is done. One can make these great promises of God not to come to pass by their act of disobedience to God's commandments. God's part is ever constant, but man is inconsistent in his ways.

If we do our part of being faithful to Him in all our endeavors, then we can be absolutely sure that goodness and mercy shall follow us all the days of our lives, and I pray that shall be our portion in Jesus's name!

How do your behaviors show God that you desire to see his Glory unfold in your life?

Pink Lemonade

Week 18

Topic: It Will End In Praise

"And We Know That All Things Work Together For Good To Them That Love God, To Them Who Are Called According To His Purpose."

Romans 8:28

Today is one of those days. I don't feel so good, so I did not make it to church. It bothers me when I cannot make it there. Despite how I may feel, I always manage to push myself through. No matter what a believer is experiencing, the circumstances will strengthen and not destroy him. Don't forget our good shepherd said He would neither leave us nor forsake us; therefore, whatever we face on earth, it is to bring the best out of us, plus it is making us a better Christian.

In the scripture, God said all things work together for good to them who love God; it means any challenges we are going through is not to pull us down but to pull us up into our next level. No champion is not challenged; Because they were challenged, they emerged as a champion. Deal with the challenges in your career pursuit, education, marriage, and life in general, and you will surely emerge a champion in Jesus's name.

Challenges are for your good and progress, never give up on God because He's working out the best for you, and you will soon share your testimony. You are blessed!

Pink Lemonade

How do you respond to unfortunate circumstances? Explain.

Pink Lemonade

Week 19

Topic: He Is Our Shield

"What Shall We Then Say To These Things? If God Is For Us, Who Can Be Against Us?" Romans 8:31

Today I feel like I am coming out of the woods from last week's chemotherapy treatment that left me so sick. Although I get very sick after having my treatments. I refuse to give in! My God is a healer and if I hold out, he will bring me out.

If we make God our shepherd, no power of darkness can be against us as we journey through life. The scripture teaches us that if God is for us, who shall be against us? The writer's perspective is not that no one will be against us, but that love will win. Did you know that you are the only person that can allow hate to come into your life and affect you? No one else can do that you except you.

Are your actions pleasing to God? Are you serving Him wholeheartedly?

Pink Lemonade

Week 20

Topic: Give Thanks

"In Everything, Give Thanks: For This Is God's Will In Christ Jesus Concerning You."

1 Thessalonians 5:18

Throughout this process, God has blessed me to continue to care for my family. Experiencing the love of my husband and three sons have been a blessing.

Daily giving of thanks always pleases God, and it brings Him great delight. As a believer, nothing should move us or make our faith dangling, but we should learn to give thanks always.

God is aware of us because he said he would neither leave us nor forsake us; thus, it allows us to know that whatever happens to believe God is aware of the circumstances. He said we should give him thanks for all things, so let us understand God, which results in us complaining less.

1 Thessalonians 5:18 teaches that by the giving of thanks, we are doing His will. Praise God!

Pink Lemonade

Are you giving thanks, or are you complaining? Choose between God's will and your will. You are a blessing.

Pink Lemonade

Week 21

Topic: Fear Not

"For God Hath Not Given Us The Spirit Of Fear, But Of Power And Love, And Of A Sound Mind."

2 Timothy 1:17

During my illness, I've experienced so many ailments! Today is one of the days I'm beyond nauseated even after wearing a patch and taking two different prescriptions! This, too, shall pass.

Fear is of the devil; the spirit of fear is not from God, because God said He had not given us the spirit of fear. So believers are not to be fearful, but they possess a daring spirit, a spirit that dares the evil.

The spirit God has given us is of power, love, and sound mind because all these are God's nature. We also are supposed to possess them.

Do you exercise faith over fear? Explain?

Pink Lemonade

Week 22

Topic: The Way

"Jesus Answered: "I Am The Way And The Truth And The Life, And No One Comes To The Father Except Through Me."

John 14:16

Today, I went in to get some scans and an EKG! It's incredible how you can meet people, and they pour so much love into you. It makes you feel so good, almost forgetting that you're sick! I'm so thankful for the love that stands the test of time. God's love is omnipotent, and it will always stand. Because of this, we must understand that Jesus is love, and the only way to experience the Father's unwavering love is through him.

If one wants to know the Father, they must come through Jesus Christ; no other way is given to man to know God except through Jesus. There is no name, no religion under the earth, in heaven can save except our belief in Jesus Christ; You cannot know the Father except you come through Jesus.

Pink Lemonade

Have you experienced knowing Jesus? How did your experience feel?

Pink Lemonade

Week 23

Topic: No Righteousness In Man

"For All Have Sinned And Fallen Short Of The Glory Of God."

Romans 3:23

Sitting here reminiscing on my younger days and being reminded of the things my mother and grandmother would say into each life, some rain will fall, but after each storm, the "Son" will shine! I know that this just a testimony for sure, and indeed the "Son" will shine again.

Every man and woman created by God are sinners by nature through the sin of disobedience by Adam in the garden of Eden. This had exposed the creatures to be in darkness, bondages as against the plan of God for humanity. The sin of Adam had made humanity to fall short of God's glory. It is important to know that no man is free from the nature of sin until we acknowledge this; there will always be war in our body and thought.

But the good news is that Jesus has come to pay the price for my sin and your sin, thus bringing us back into the former relationship we had with God before, but note it is not on your worth, but the worth of Jesus Christ praise God! If you have not accepted Jesus into your life, you remain a sinner, the old nature which every man born of Adam had is still set work with you, and you need Jesus to get reconnected again to God.

Are you saved, or are you a religious person? Make the right choices, which results in eternal life.

Pink Lemonade

Week 24

Topic: Saved by Grace

"For By Grace, You Have Been Saved Through Faith. And This Is Not Your Doing; It Is The Gift Of God". Ephesians 2:8

Although this is a hard test for me, I never fail to thank God for his goodness because I know so many people going through tough situations. Only the Grace of God makes us a saint; it gives us right standing with God. Apostle Paul teaches: "I am what I am by the Grace of God." The same with us believers; Grace saves us. It is not by our works or righteousness. We are what and who we are by His grace.

Believers should have the mindset that it is by the Grace of God; they achieved whatever height they have attained in life. Such a mindset will help to humble them and take life with all simplicity.

Do you believe that what you have is by Grace, or you think it is your power? Give him thanks for all, and He will do more for us. Glory be to God.

Pink Lemonade

Week 25

Topic: You Are The Best

"I Praise You Because I Am Fearfully And Wonderfully Made; Your Works Are Wonderful, I Know That Full Well."

Psalm 139:14

Today, my son asked me: "Do you need me to do anything for you?" I responded: "Just stick by me while I am going through." He assured me that he would do whatever it takes to make this process as easy as possible. It made me feel so good to hear him say those words to me because my soul felt a very positive lift!

Everything God created is perfect, excellent, and beautiful. The Bible states in Genesis: "Behold, all He created, and He said they are all good."

God created you and I perfectly and beautifully. He created us in His image, so learn to accept what God said about you, not what people say.

God loves us, He created you well, and He made you with the best of material, so get excited about yourself! You are the best, you are wonderful and created in God's image, regardless of the battles life brings, you are created in His image. Hallelujah!

How do your actions show that you have confidence that you are wonderfully and fearfully made?

Pink Lemonade

Week 26

Topic: Love God Totally

"Love The Lord Your God With All Of Your Heart And With All Your Soul And With All Your Strength." Deuteronomy 6:5

I am elated because of all the support I have gotten and continue to receive. My sister (only sister) has such a motherly nature that gives me such comfort. Although my mother is no longer here, I feel her presence anytime I am with my sister.

Believers are to love God with all their heart, soul, plus all their strength. This means loving God at the peak. Nothing should take God's place in our hearts but love him wholeheartedly, which comes with a great blessing. When we love God, we will obey his commandment. We will love humanity and eschew evil in all ramifications. It is so important if we are to receive any blessing from God.

Don't love God midway, but love Him with all your heart. That is how to walk and receive from GOD. If you are neither cold nor hot, God said He wills sprue you out of His mouth, as this is many Christians today. I pray thy Lord will deliver you from look warmness in the spirit in Jesus' name.

Do you love God? Then serve Him with the whole of your heart. You are a blessing!

Pink Lemonade

Week 27

Topic: Be Selfless

"Love Your Neighbors As Yourself."

Matthew 22:39

Week 27

I met an older woman while having chemotherapy today. I complimented her because although she has no hair like many of us who are doing chemotherapy treatments, she is still so beautiful. She then proceeded to tell me this is her third time-fighting cancer over four years. I have come to realize that I am beyond blessed and that there is always someone who has it worse than you.

The extent to which we love ourselves, we are to love our neighbors like that. God is love; that is why He sent his only begotten son to die for the world's sin. Love is the answer to all law; if you love genuinely, you have fulfilled the law.

We are to reflect our Father's nature as a son; God is love let us love in return, who are we to love? God's creature. If all humanity would embrace God's teaching, our nation will be a better place to live.

Do not give it to others what you will not accept. May God help us to love genuinely in Jesus' name!

How do you exemplify gladness and joy despite what is going on around or even inside of you? Do your actions reflect your faith? Explain.

_____
_____
_____
_____
_____
_____
_____
_____
_____
_____
_____
_____
_____
_____
_____
_____

Pink Lemonade

Week 28

Topic: Say It To God

"Do Not Be Anxious About Anything, But In Every Situation, By Prayer And Petition, With Thanksgiving, Present Your Request To God. Philippians 4:6

Having been diagnosed took a huge toll on me but having the best team of doctors and oncologists on my side made me feel as if I was in the best hands possible. Thank God for genuine and compassionate people, especially when you need it.

As believers, the world's worries should not affect us because when and if they do, we cannot communicate effectively with God. Our relationship will be hindered. God desires that we do not get worried about our circumstances but instead present those things to God in prayer, thanksgiving, and supplication. You are sure to receive answers to those situations.

Don't forget he had assured us that we would answer us before we call, and while we are not yet speaking, he will answer us. So brethren take that issue to God in prayer and stop complaining. God listens to us when we pray. So pray!

Pink Lemonade

How often do you pray? Explain.

Pink Lemonade

Week 29

Topic: Peace And Understanding

"And The Peace Of God Which Transcends All Understanding Will Guard Your Heart And Your Mind In Christ Jesus!

Philippians 4:7

Growing up, I watched my mom multi-task so much until I made it my business to do the very same thing. It makes life a lot simpler whenever I can juggle more than one thing at a time. There is no way with all going on to let this take charge of my world. Thank you, God, for making me who I am!

Anyone in Christ Jesus has the Peace of God that no man can explain; that is, the peace that surpasses all understanding, and it becomes ours the moment we accept Jesus into our life.

It is only in Christ that we can claim this Peace of God, which will lead our hearts and minds as we continue in the race of life. Note money does not guarantee genuine peace, your wealth, connections, or affiliations does not guarantee it. Peace is only granted when we are in Jesus Christ, our savior. So, embrace him today and have everlasting joy, Peace is your portion in Jesus name.

Do you see the Peace of God exemplified in your life? If so, explain.

Pink Lemonade

Week 30

Topic: His Word Is Sharper

"Every Word Of God Proves True: He Is A Shield To Those Who Take Refuge In Him."

Proverbs 30:5

    God's Word is real, true, and powerful to those who believe; His Word is a shield to them that have faith in him. Every Word of the scripture is to teach us. You cannot reap the treasure in the Word until you learn to treasure what it teaches us to do. You may ask: "How do I treasure God's Word?" Read the Bible, believe in what the scriptures say and run with it in your mind that his Word will never fail and cannot fail, that is how to make it work. God's Word is a refuge o those that take refuge in it and believe in it.

Pink Lemonade

Do you believe God's Word?

Pink Lemonade

Week 31

Topic: Do All To Honor God

"So Whether You Eat Or Drink Or Whatever You Do, Do It All For God's Glory."

1 Corinthians 10:31

Today I met a young woman who has a similar diagnosis. She shared her doctor's projected plans for treatment with me, which seemed or sounded easier than mines. I reflected on what my doctor warned me about, all treatments will not be the same, although your diagnosis may be the same. I learned early on to appreciate this because God's timing is not ours, his thoughts are not like ours, and his ways are not like our ways.

Whatever we achieve here on earth, we need to return all glory to God, the giver of all things. When you have food to eat, thank Him for the provision. Thank God for all things, big and small.

Glory: do not forget that God will not share His glory with anyone. When we fail to give him the glory due to unto him, it means we are proud. We, as children of God, should always be humble and give God the thanks. We should serve him in the spirit of humility, knowing that we are unworthy. Praise God!

Pink Lemonade

Give an example of something you did that shows you serve God in the spirit of humility?

Pink Lemonade

Week 32

Topic: Be Orderly In Your Approach

"In The Beginning, God Created The Heaven And The Earth."

Genesis 1:1

When I find the time, I like to read Bible stories that uplift and encourage me. Stories of the Bible are reminders that God will see us through. Our God is a God of process. He plans everything before embarking on it.

The scripture states that before God started creating man, He created the Heaven and the earth.

God is orderly, and I know that he designed my husband for me. I am most thankful for the love and support for my husband; he never made me feel less of who I am because of my hair loss or surgery.

What have you done lately to show those whom God has blessed you to call family how much you appreciate them?

Pink Lemonade

Week 33

Topic: Proclaim His Glory

"The Heavens Declare The Glory Of God; The Skies Proclaim The Work Of His Hands."

Psalm 19:1

Everything God created is purposed to praise and honor His name. In our text, the scripture said the heavens proclaim the Glory of God, the skies plus all the works of His hands. The Bible states: "Let everything that has breath praise His holy name;" thus, all living and the nonliving should praise His name, praise God!

How do we declare the glory of God? Through our deed in every place, we find ourselves and the fruit of our lips always praising Him.

Are you displaying His glory in the wrong way or in a righteous way? God is watching you!

Pink Lemonade

Week 34

Topic: He Knows

"The Lord Knows The Way Of The Righteous, But The Way Of The Wicked Will Perish.

Psalm 1:6

For me decorating relieves stress. The week before I had my surgery (four days prior), I was able to work and decorate a huge wedding and took my mind off of the stress. The colors were teal green, gold, and ivory and came together very well.

The Lord promised his children that He would neither leave nor forsake them; therefore, their ways are not hidden to Him. God has us in the palm of His hand. They will never be put to shame or destroyed by enemies because He watches over them.

In further detail, God said the wicked way would surely perish because God's mercy has departed from them unless they repent and accept Jesus. God is daily angry with the wicked. I want to believe you are not part of the wicked? Because the wicked shall suddenly be destroyed. Nothing is hidden from God, He knows all, and mainly He watches over the saints. Praise Jesus!

God is daily angry with the wicked. I want to believe you are not part of the wicked. How do you separate yourself from ungodliness?

Pink Lemonade

Week 35

Topic: You Are Mine

"Thus Says The Lord Fear Not, For I Have Redeemed You: I Have Called You By Name, You Are Mine.."

Isaiah 43:1

Have you ever felt as if you needed a place of belonging? Well, today, that was me. Life is ever-changing. Loved ones transition to glory, new babies arrive, our children grow up into men and women. To be stable, we must find solace in Jesus and know that he remains the same, although life changes.

Although today my emotions are everywhere, I recollected my thoughts, pulled myself together, and realized that I should not fear. There is nothing that you are going through that is strange to God. He understands. Stay faithful to Him and serve Him, and soon God will come through for you praise God.

What experience have you encountered that served as a reminder that you belong to God?

___

Pink Lemonade

Week 36

Topic: Only He Is God

"I Am The Lord, And Besides Me, There Is No Savior."

Isaiah 43:11

No power, no blood, no name can redeem a man from his sin except the name and the blood of Jesus. Besides Him, there is no savior. Jesus is the way the truth and the life.

Have you accepted Jesus? If not, today is your day of salvation. Accept Him and be blessed here on earth and in eternity. Praise God!

Have you accepted Jesus? If not, today is your day of salvation. Accept Him and be blessed here on earth and in eternity. Praise God!

Pink Lemonade

Week 37

Topic: You Are The Light

"Ye Are The Light Of The World. A City That Is Set On A Hill Cannot Be Hidden".

Mathew 5:14

Believers in Christ Jesus are the light of the world; they are created to add salt to the world and humanity in general. They are the light that shines in the dark.

The question now is: "How does God's grace lighten up our world? Are we contributing to the darkness of this world?" God's standards about who he wants us to be are not hidden, so let us ensure that we add value to our world, let us represent light in whatever area we find ourselves. Love what God loves and hate what He hates, and as we do this, our light will never be hidden in life.

Pink Lemonade

How will you be the light?

Pink Lemonade

Week 38

Topic: Shine Your Light

"Let Your Light So Shine Before Men, That They May See Your Good Works, And Glorify Your Father Which Is In Heaven."

Mathew 5:16

God commands believers that we should let our light shine before men, that they may see your Father's good works; anytime we do good works, we reflect the nature and glory of Christ. Anytime we do this, God is highly pleased with us.

Do you know that we can win people to Christ through Our actions, so let us watch our behavior. If possible, ask yourself: "Is my action drawing people to Christ or chasing them?"

Are you a blessing or a lesson to your world? Answer that question genuinely and take the necessary steps.

Pink Lemonade

Week 39

Topic: Seek The Kingdom

"Seek Ye First The Kingdom Of God And His Righteousness And All These Things Shall Be Added Unto You."

Mathew 6:33

First, we are created by God to serve Him. We are created to enhance, project, and impact our world. The essence of God creating us is to seek the Kingdom, and this came with a promise that all our needs shall be met, so service to God ensures that all your earthly need plus your spiritual needs are met.

I have seen many turning after mundane things of this world instead of seeking how they will please God. Make God your priority, His service, and other things that will help project God's Kingdom, and He had promised us that all our needs shall be met.

Is God a priority to you? Explain.

Pink Lemonade

Week 40

Topic: Be Rich In The Word

"Let The Word Of Christ Dwell In You Richly In All Wisdom; Teaching And Admonishing One Another In Psalm And Hymns And Spiritual Songs, Singing With Grace In Your Heart To The Lord."

Colossians 3:16

Long Suffering is important as a Believer. God's Word is precious, real, and powerful; therefore, we are advised to let it dwell richly in us. We should teach others about God's Word.

Psalms, Spiritual Songs, and Hymns connect the church in Heaven to the church on earth. We can grow through Psalms, Spiritual Songs, and Hymns. The scripture teaches us that we should not give room to complain in any form but to serve God and be grateful.

Pink Lemonade

How are we to teach ourselves through Psalms, Spiritual Songs, and Hymns?

Pink Lemonade

Week 41

Topic: He Changed Not

"Jesus Christ The Same Yesterday And Today And Forever."

Hebrews 13:8

Our God remains the only unchanging God in Heaven and on earth. He never changes. He said before creating the world: "I am that I am."

The text allows us to know that Jesus is the same yesterday, today, and forever.

Whatever miracles he has performed in the past, He can do again even in our time. Our savior is Jesus Christ; He remains forever. His love is unchanging.

In what ways have you recognized in your life that God was God, and continues to God? Explain.

Pink Lemonade

Week 42

Topic: Mount Up Like An Eagle

"They That Wait Upon The Lord Shall Renew Their Strength; They Shall Mount Up With Wings As Eagles; They Shall Run And Not Be Weary: They Shall Walk And Not Faint."

Isaiah 40:31

It is a good thing to wait upon the Lord. When we wait, we are not wasting our time or losing anything destined for us to obtain; however, when we wait, we are waiting for God to show His mighty power over our situation.

Let me sound this clearly: Those who cannot wait are not fit for this kingdom race. God takes us through all the classes of life lessons before dropping our breakthrough in our hands.

The waiting period is training time, preparation time, plus a period of mentoring. You can compare waiting to take a class. If you enroll in a course, you are supposed to study pass. So it is with God that you should want to learn the lesson you are being taught through your experiences and endeavors. It is no one's aimed goal to fail. But if we fail, which we often do, he will help us learn to wait on Him!

Pink Lemonade

> Are you patient as God works in your life? How do you apply what you learn through spiritual lessons to your life?

Pink Lemonade

Week 43

Topic: Peace Of God

"Peace I Leave With You: My Peace I Give You. Do Not Be Afraid."

John 14:27

Have you ever felt afraid? We all have, so you are not alone. God's Word teaches us that we have Peace in Jesus Christ; therefore, do not let your heart be troubled. Do all within your power to ensure that nothing or no one takes your peace or joy. Nothing in this world should be strong enough to take away the peace, which Christ has purchased for you.

Do you believe you have Peace In Jesus' name? Explain.

Pink Lemonade

Week 44

Topic: Commit All To Him

"Commit Your Way To The Lord: Trust In Him, And He Will Do This: He Will Make Your Righteous Reward Shine Like The Dawn."

Psalm 37:4

It is a good thing to commit to God for direction, leading, and success in one way.

When we commit our ways to God, let us also trust in Him to bring it to pass, because some commit their ways to God but never trust God to bring it to pass, that is a failure even before setting out.

To God, they are still full of panic, fear uncertainty. No, no, no, that is not how to trust God.

Yours is to commit and trust Him, leave the doing part for God.

Note when you claim you trust Him for something rest totally, no doubt, but total belief in God's supremacy to do it.

Do you have a sense of restfulness once you have submitted all circumstances to the Lord?

Pink Lemonade

Week 45

Topic: Ask In His Name

"Ask, And You Will Receive That Your Joy May Be Full."

John 16:24B

In Christianity, we ask before we receive from God if we fail to ask, we will never receive from God. That is why prayer is key in the life of a believer.

According to our text today, God advises us to ask until our joy is full; until you see it happen, don't stop asking God. So what God wants from us is that we should do anything that will enhance your faith life and things that will make you enjoy the best of God on earth so that your joy and Peace will be intact.

Let us continuously ask God for whatever our needs are. He has them sufficiently, do not look another way around but look unto Him for he cares for you and will neither leave you nor forsake you. Glory!

Pink Lemonade

How do you see God working in your life as your provider? Explain.

Pink Lemonade

Week 46

Topic: He Loves You

"For God So Loved The World That He Gave His Only Begotten Son, That Whosoever Believes In Him Should Not Perish, But Have Everlasting Life."

John 3:16

No matter how dirty you may feel, Jesus loves you! No matter how unworthy you may think you are, he died for you to be saved! God has you in mind. That is why He died for the sin of the world.

The scripture states that we are saved if we believe. He said: "believe." So your salvation is hanged on your belief system.

Pink Lemonade

Do you believe that Jesus is the son of God? Do you think He is sent of God to liberate humanity from his dark life and sin? The day you believe does the day of your salvation come.

Pink Lemonade

Week 47

Topic: Love One Another

"Beloved, Let Us Love One Another, For Love Is God, And Everyone Who Loves Is Born Of God And Knows God.

1 John 4:7

God is love, and we too must love in return. God loved us from the beginning. The scripture states: "For God commanded his love towards us, in that while we are yet a sinner he died for us." Praise God! God loves us dearly, and He wants us to love him in return and also love humanity.

Everyone who loves is a child of God and knows God; Anytime you show love to God and humanity, you are a child of God.

Let us love indeed and not in word alone. Everything about Jesus is love, and if we love, we have fulfilled the law. Hallelujah!

Do you operate in love at all times? Explain.

Pink Lemonade

Week 48

Topic: Motivate One Another

"Let Us Think Of Ways To Motivations Another To Acts Of Love And Good Works."

Hebrew 10:24

As believers, we are to add value to humanity, motivate people to do good work through our actions. The scripture teaches that we are the light of the world. So we should light up our world, let others see God's light in you, and give glory to your Father in Heaven.

Let us encourage people to do good work eschew evil; this has a great reward from God. Praise God!

You are a mentor to somebody; someone is observing you and following after your footstep, so be extra careful.

Pink Lemonade

Are you motivating people to good work or bad work? Explain.

Pink Lemonade

Week 49

Topic: Think On The Word

"Finally Brothers And Sisters Whatever Is True, Whatever Is Noble, Whatever Is Right, Whatever Is Pure, Whatever Is Lovely, Whatever Is Admirable, If Anything Is Excellent Or Praiseworthy Think About Such Things."

Philippians 4:8

    As children of God, we are only permitted to think about what is pure, good, praiseworthy, and excellent. God has given us direction on what we should pattern our thinking on. He did not advise that we pattern it after the mundane things of this world. But think about things that bring Glory to his Holy name. Think much about righteousness, and your light will continue to shine.

Godly things carry virtues and will enhance your faith. You are to think about such things. Praise God!

Are you focused on Heaven and Heavenly things, although being occupied with the cares of this world? Explain.

Pink Lemonade

Week 50

Topic: Obedience To God

"If They Obey And Serve Him, They Will Spend The Rest Of Their Days In Prosperity And Their Years In Contentment."

Job 36:11

Obedience to the Word of God is the gateway to prosperity and abundance. If you follow God's Word as given in the scripture, your light will shine for all to see. Disobedience to God's Word is the root of a human's problem.

The scripture states that if they obey and serve God, we must abide by believing all of his words as revealed in the scripture and through serving Him. What God has revealed to you, you must share with others and serve God with it. If you obey and do not help, you are still disobedient to God; You must fully be obedient to God's commandments to reciprocate blessings as a child of God.

Pink Lemonade

In what ways do you obey and serve God?

Pink Lemonade

Week 51

Topic: A New Life

"Forget The Former Things: Do Not Dwell On The Past: See I Am Doing A New Thing."

Isaiah 48:18-19A

    The Word of God is teaching us that we should let our past go! Do not keep thinking about negatives things from yesterday anymore. God is set to do a new thing in your life; In fact, he said: "I am doing a new thing, so let your past be your past and hold on to this God who has begun thing in your life."

    If a man is in Christ Jesus, old things are gone. Begin to work in the newness of life and see your life-changing for good in Jesus' name. You should be excited about life.

Do not allow anything to trouble your heart. God is manifesting in your life in Jesus' name.

Pink Lemonade

Week 52

Topic: Praise Him

"Let Everything That Has Breath Praise The Lord: Praise The Lord.

Psalm 160:6

Praising God is a commandment from God. God created humanity for praise, not for any other thing but constant praise. What we do in praising God is that we are exalting his Holy name for all he has done, therefore making him do more for us.

When we praise God, we extended our invitation to him to do more for us praising him is the only food we can give unto our God for all he has done for us, and you know one thing? God said: "He inhabited the praises of his children". Hallelujah!

Any time we are praising God, God does come down bodily, he will not send an angel, He will come down by himself, and you know what that means? He will give answers to all our prayer requests plus delivering us from all oppression of the devil. You can pray amidst, but you can't praise amidst. Praise God!

The Holy Spirit is a Gift from God to us. While the Holy Spirit is a keeper of those who want to be kept it is also a mediator between God and man. What does this mean to you? This is constant assurance that despite where you go, God is with you.

Pink Lemonade

Conclusion

Lamp To My Feet

"Your Word Is A Lamp To My Feet And A Light For My Path."

Psalm 119:105

Life will have dark moments. There is no doubt about it being so; however, we can choose how we deal with dark moments. For example, David referred to God's Word as a lamp, the giver of direction, way maker, and a light to his part in life. It behooves us to do the same during our most troublesome moments. Lean and depend on the Lord and his promises.

When we truly cherish the Word of God and believe in it, it will always guide us in all our actions in life and destiny. If you do not have faith in the Word of God, it cannot work for you; it will not become your reality. The Word of God gives directions, it lightens up every area of darkness in our life, and it paves the way for our upliftment in life, it also makes us victorious over every situation and circumstances of life.

When we as the children of God have scriptures richly dwelling in us, and we believe in it dearly, it makes us not to sin against God.

In conclusion, let us take in God's Word. It will continue to lighten up every part of darkness in our lives and ensure that we do not fall. God will lead us through the Holy Spirit as we learn to believe all His promises. Always use God's Word as a sweetener whenever life throws you lemons and make the best *Pink Lemonade!*

Made in the USA
Columbia, SC
29 March 2025